My Side of Depression

By Don Legun

A Righter Book

Cover Illustration by the author

Righter Publishing Company, Inc.
PO Box 105
Timberlake, North Carolina 27583

www.righterbooks.com

April, 2009

Printed and bound in the United States
of America

Library of Congress Control Number
2009925873

ISBN: 978-1-934936-26-9
My Side of Depression
By Don Legun

Author's Biography

Don Legun's depression began in 1989 and he has lived with it ever since. His experiences and personal insight have helped many people understand and live with this disease.

Prior to his depression, he coached gymnastics and taught high school industrial arts. When Legun was given the opportunity to fly, he changed careers and went through Aviation Officer Candidate School and started a 10-year naval career. He earned his wings and was twice deployed to the Middle East flying the Navy A-6 Intruder.

His next naval assignment was teaching sales, marketing and management for the Officer Recruiting Command. Then the USS Independence, CV-61, found him and his responsibility changed to planning flight operations for the deployed air wing.

Following the stint in the Navy, he created and owned a windsurfing/kite retail store where he developed and taught an award-winning "Learn to Windsurf" school. Legun also volunteered time teaching principles of flight to school children using kites.

Wishing to accompany his wife on her corporate moves, he eventually closed the store. When she started working out-of-the-home and the children moved out, roots were established on a lake in North Carolina. Legun spent five years building the custom home where they now live.

As it neared completion, he invented a computerized switch, for which he holds the patent. Currently he keeps busy building, designing, and inventing, with an occasional time out for writing.

Dedication

This book is dedicated to my wonderful wife. As she fought for my survival, she was my advocate, my coach, my strength, my teacher and my love. When I look back on those dark times, I am amazed at her patience and personal strength, which guided me out of that darkness. To this day, she supports me in all that I do and has been a huge influence on publishing this story. Without her, I wouldn't be here and this story would never have been told.

This book is dedicated to Becky, my special wife and everlasting love. Thank you for helping me choose life over death.

Don

Introduction

The numbers of young, tragic suicides have driven me to write this book in an effort to educate people about my disease called depression. I've tried to target three groups.

First are those who either are with or will be with someone depressed. I want to help provide understanding in order to prevent a situation from escalating and then encourage everyone to learn more than what this book provides.

Second are those who have depression. When you have it, you don't usually recognize it in yourself. You know something is wrong but don't know what it is and what to do. I'm trying to provide some answers and direction. So if depressed, you will understand that you are not alone.

Third are those who have been close to someone who took his/her own life. Without understanding this disease, there can be guilt. I'm hoping this book will better provide the answer to "Why?"

There is a lot of anger that goes on inside the mind of a depressed person. That anger can turn to rage. When it rises to that level, it can be held internally, leading to suicide or it may go external leading to murder. I'm providing tools that will help the observer recognize early stages of depression and prevent escalation to that point where it is dangerous. Many of our military personnel and their families are facing problems of depression with no tools to help. I'm trying to offer one.

I've had clinical depression for over 16 years. The insights I've gained from looking suicide square in the face have provided comfort to many. I've shared thoughts and experiences that have helped my friends and family deal with this disease either for themselves or their friends. This book has been written because those with whom I've shared my story have encouraged me to publish it. It has been written with a great deal of honesty and passion.

I am not a doctor or psychologist and the information I've provided is my insight based upon my experiences. It has not been approved or supported by any medical or psychological organization.

My Side of Depression

This book will hopefully help shed some light on something most people don't want to talk about, depression. I want to share my story and give some insights as to how to recognize depression and what to do, whether you see it in yourself or someone you know.

What is depression?

Books will tell you that the following behaviors or feelings are signs of depression:

- Constant sadness (crying)
- Irritability
- Hopelessness
- Trouble sleeping
- Low energy or fatigue
- Feeling worthless or guilty for no reason
- Significant weight change
- Difficulty concentrating
- Loss of interest in favorite activities

These are good indicators of depression. Friends and family may be able to recognize some of these symptoms. However, it might only be the depressed person who would recognize these traits within her/himself.

What It's Like

My emotions became like open wounds and I was over-sensitive to just about any situation and over-reacted to just about anything. Little problems were monumental. I would actually feel emotional pain when I heard laughter. I'd be angry and jealous because I wanted to be happy like those around me, but my body wouldn't let me. The depression took that emotion from me.

I would feel separated from everyone else as if I were in a box on a shelf. I could see and hear what was going on around me but I couldn't interact. When I did try, the results were bad mostly because the information coming into my brain became skewed.

An example would be like being on a football team. A play goes to the right and you know that, but being out of control of your mind, you go left. You become angry with yourself because you know better and you know your action affects those around you. The team becomes angry with you because they don't understand why you're not doing what you're supposed to do. You can't control your actions and so you want to hide. As the Southwest Airlines commercial says, "You want to get away?"

Well, I did hide and then people didn't understand why I was hiding, which made me want to hide even more. I went on long drives to keep from being home when the kids arrived and I wouldn't answer the telephone. Sometimes my wife would come home and find me in the closet of a dark room. All I wanted was, "Leave me alone!" I knew I wasn't me. I didn't know why and I knew the people around me didn't understand. All I wanted was for them to let me go to my room. I wanted to sleep the whole thing away hoping to wake up from a bad dream.

With that skewed mind, I believed I was the cause of everything wrong. I perceived that I was hurting all the people around me when in fact I wasn't. They wanted to help, but they didn't understand what was happening to me and they didn't know what to do. I was hurting them and I knew it, but had no control, no ability, to stop the hurt no matter how much I wanted to stop it. All things that would usually bring me joy now brought me hurt because there was no joy in them anymore. And if the things that formerly gave me joy now didn't, was I ever going to find joy or happiness anywhere? This is when suicide entered my thoughts. In my skewed mind, it was the only logical out.

My thinking was that I would finally quit feeling the pain of not being in control of my emotions. Those emotions were getting worse with time and the chance of escaping that pain was getting farther and farther away. I felt like suicide would rid me of these demons. It made sense that with me gone, I'd be relieving all the people around me of the pain that I thought I was causing them.

Of course, the truth was my death would create more pain for those around me because they would blame themselves for my death. So suicide is a flawed thought. A depressed mind has messed-up thought processes and what is perceived as help might be and probably is just the opposite.

I understood how taking my life would affect the ones I loved and that was the only thing that kept me from following through with my thoughts. It was an internal battle that is impossible to describe. It was right fighting wrong, good battling evil, all happening inside my body, inside my brain.

Cause of Depression – My Theory

Everyone has a different tolerance to emotional trauma. However, no matter what that tolerance is, it has limitations. In a sense, you can deplete the very thing that helps you cope, giving you that tolerance. The neurotransmitters are what provide the reasoning capabilities. The more trauma there is, the more the neurotransmitters are reduced. I believe the body has a way of replenishing those chemicals, but at different rates for different people. Trauma is a vague word and so I've tried to break it down a little farther. Everyone has different morals--what is right and what is wrong. When your morals become wronged, or when something happens to you that you would never do or wish upon someone else, you become traumatized. This would be a very deep passion but ultimately you feel wronged through no fault of your own. There seems no justification for a painful event happening to you and you can see no escape from the emotions you're experiencing.

My Story Part 1

How does anyone get depression? I can trace mine to a specific set of circumstances. Based upon the previous information, let's see if you can find the source of depression in my story.

When I was an officer in the Navy, I sent in a letter of resignation after almost 10 years of good times, good experiences and good memories. When an officer wants to become a civilian again, he must turn in a formal letter of resignation and timing is critical. If it's too soon, the people working with him will know he's leaving and they can make life difficult. Submitting too late and he is obligated to the next three-year tour of duty.

While at sea on an aircraft carrier going from Philadelphia around South America to San Diego, I submitted my letter in what I thought was the proper time frame. After waiting two weeks, it was denied. I resubmitted and it was denied again. The third submission was also denied but this time with an explanation. The application instructions for resignation had changed without my knowledge and now I would have to spend another year on the ship. This devastating event happened while I was working 20-hour days in a high-stress position.

The ship finally pulled into San Diego, but because of a new job promotion, my wife was waiting for me in Des Moines, Iowa. I felt I had done everything I should have and expected to be released from the Navy based upon the instructions that I had known for quite some time. I had worked extremely hard giving much more than what was required. When the Navy wouldn't let me leave, I felt this was terribly unfair. It was an injustice. I would never do anything like that to anybody else and it was hard to accept that I would be on the ship away from my family for another year.

That was the beginning. Due to cost, I had to live on the ship, which in itself is stressful. While in port, workers chipped paint and non-skid 24 hours per day. It was like living inside a steel drum with somebody banging on the outside. Along with that physical stress, came the emotional. I was tasked by my new incoming boss to physically redo the office space. My outgoing boss didn't want anything changed until he left. So every time the incoming boss came by, I was chewed out for not getting anything done. He didn't care about the outgoing boss; he wanted the task done by the time he got there. All of these were no-win situations.

Each one of these situations individually would depress anybody and that type of depression is one that most people can resolve. For me, it was the cumulative effect of all the situations that drove me into the beginning of depression. I was angry at my situation and I couldn't cope with it. My only release was to get away from the environment. I took long drives to escape. On one of those drives, I broke out in uncontrollable crying. This could probably be called the despair stage.

I called my wife and she encouraged me to come home where I saw a psychologist and worked on cognitive therapy. Feeling better, I went back to the ship and back into the same problem. I quickly recognized that I needed to leave the situation. To make that happen, I saw my first psychiatrist, a military doctor. I was diagnosed with depression and was ordered off the ship to a less stressful job. It was the only way that I could quickly remove myself from the situation that made me depressed. Weeks later my resignation came through and I joined my wife in Des Moines. This part of my life began my depression. In time it got worse.

My Story Part 2

When out of that situation, I felt almost normal and this seemed a good time to start a business. With no real symptoms of depression, I poured my heart and soul into a retail venture. Long hours of planning and working seven days per week paid off and I doubled my business every year. I knew a lot of people and became somewhat of a celebrity with the local radio and TV stations.

Then my wife received a job transfer and everything changed. The distance between our new home and the store was too great and I had to close the store. This became a very tough time for me because there wasn't much left in my body to handle a depressing situation after the Navy episode. I describe this stage of my life like finding a dog, raising, nurturing, loving and training it for three years and then taking it out behind the shed and shooting it. It was devastating.

During this time I had a close-out sale and the people I thought were friends (people I had helped for years) didn't want to pay the reduced price I needed to keep from loosing money. They expected me to give away the merchandize. So not only did I have to kill my investment of three years, it felt like my friends became jackals, kicking me while I was down. Again, I felt this was an immoral injustice and I would never do anything like that to anybody else.

This drove me into a deep depression and for the first time my family saw me sick. I became suicidal and remember planning my death. Through love, frustration, patience and understanding, my wife encouraged me to see a psychiatrist. I was again diagnosed with clinical depression and for the first time, medication was prescribed.

My Story Part 3

You would think that would be the end of it, but I had more to learn. My wife was transferred to the Research Triangle and because the medication made me feel almost normal, I thought this would be a good time to pursue the mechanical engineering degree that I always wanted. I enrolled in some courses at Wake Tech to catch me up with what I needed to go to NC State. I knew to be competitive in the job market at my age; I would need straight As. This added just a bit of pressure. I took Comp-1 (retake for bad grade), Calc-1 and Intro to Chemistry. All went well and I got the As that I needed. It took a strong effort but it worked for me. So during the next quarter I took Calc-2, Chemistry-1 and Physics-1. Unfortunately, there was not enough time in the day to do all the homework necessary to achieve all As. The pressure I put on myself overloaded the medication I was taking and I blew a gasket. I couldn't do what I expected myself to do. To me, it was another immoral injustice. However, this time I brought it on myself. Although I didn't feel I was as depressed as before, I was showing signs that I was heading that way.

Because of what my wife was observing, she talked with my psychiatrist to learn what could be done. It was decided that for my safely I should be hospitalized. That would also be a good time to find the root of the depression through testing and then adjust the medication as necessary.

This is when I met a number of patients and I found out that everyone with depression had similar symptoms. I realized for the first time that I wasn't the only person who was thinking the same dark thoughts. Situations that hospitalized us were different, so why was it we all had similar thoughts? Because depression has the same symptoms, no matter who you are or how you become sick. I learned that depression was a disease and I didn't bring it upon myself.

With that new knowledge I asked fellow patients about medication. I found out everyone responds differently to different drugs. Sometimes it would take a combination of drugs to achieve the desired results. I also learned that when given medication with no counseling, my depression would gradually go away and when the medication was removed to start a different drug, my depression would come back. The pattern was always the same. That confirmed in my mind that this disease was chemically based and not just emotionally based. Although I was scared to death when I was hospitalized, it was probably one of the best learning experiences for me.

My Story Part 4

I thought my story ended with the hospital. It didn't. Recently I became very tired and I was taking two-hour naps twice a day and sleeping ten hours at night. To find out why, blood tests were done and medications were tried. Nothing seemed to work. I was told I had chronic fatigue syndrome. My doctor told me there are no drugs or cures and I'd just have to live with it.

My wife came to the rescue again. She had been reading about adrenal fatigue and noticed similarities between people who had that sickness and me. By coincidence, her gynecologist had worked with adrenal fatigue patients and as a favor; she accepted me as a patient. She tested for deficiencies down to the cellular level by using saliva instead of blood. Because of my depression, she also had my neurotransmitters tested. When the panel of results came back it showed that I was a very tired man with neurotransmitters not functioning at the level they should be.

She put me on a regiment of supplements, NOT drugs, but supplements. I figured that because I don't eat healthy foods, taking the supplements made a lot of sense.

By the end of six months, my sleep pattern was back to normal and surprisingly I gained another benefit. My original personality found its way back. The antidepressants pulled me from the depression and brought me back to about 95% of myself. With the supplements added, I felt like my old self. I gained back my confidence and stability. Without this last healing stage, this book never would have been written.

Now when people see me and ask what I've done to look so good, I simply tell them, "My gynecologist helped me." Because I'm a guy, I watch the expression on their face. As you might be able to tell, my sense of humor is back. That is a true measurement of my level of depression. Although I still have the disease, the symptoms are all but gone and I live life normally.

Chemical Connection to Depression

Depression works on the mind in a funny way. When depressed, there are chemicals in the brain (like serotonin) that don't allow the neurotransmitters in the brain to communicate as they should. I believe some of these chemicals become depleted. With time the body will replace what has been lost and you'll be back to normal. This is an example of a mild depression, something the body can handle and recover from. With clinical depression more neurotransmitters are destroyed than the body can replace. It would be like putting so much stress on the chemical supply that it runs out. When really bad, the manufacturing plant that makes these chemicals seems to break. Maybe it can be repaired and maybe it can't, but in the meantime those chemicals have to come from some where for the mind to work correctly. For me, the factory is broken and I'm pretty sure it will be for the rest of my life. I need to use chemicals to replace what my body no longer has.

In my personal story, I believe during that stressful time with the Navy, I lost most of what makes those neurotransmitters work. Without medication I was able to find my way back with therapy. If I hadn't had the Navy trauma, I might have been able to recover from the loss of my store with just therapy. But somehow with the Navy depression, there just wasn't enough of what makes the mind work to bring me back on my own. It took a chemical, a medication, to give my mind a chance to work in a way that would clear out the cobwebs and let me be myself again. At this time I believed the medication was just a bridge that would let my brain heal itself. It wasn't until I was changing medication (because of side effects) that I truly understood the chemical relationship to this disease. As I went off the medication, I could feel the depression taking over. Back with the pill, I could feel the depression start to melt away. This cycle happened at least four times in a six-month period. This was my proof that depression at this level was a chemical problem.

Depression wasn't in my head; it had my head.

Depression vs. Clinical Depression

I've talked about depression at a couple different levels. There is a depression that the body will work its way out of in a couple of days. That needs no treatment. Then there is clinical depression that will require either talk (cognitive) therapy from a psychologist or chemical therapy from a psychiatrist. It depends on how much damage your body's chemical factory has suffered.

Cognitive Therapy

When my depression started, I was able to cope with it by seeing a psychologist and using cognitive therapy. This therapy usually lasts for several months and includes many exercises that help a person recognize and process events. An example would be receiving a school paper with an F on it. A depressed mind would think, "I always get Fs" -- a very negative thought. In reality, this may be the only F received all year.

Using cognitive thinking, the student would recognize this "forever" thought and change it to something that is not lasting such as, "This has been a bad day for me for grades, but there is always tomorrow." This therapy helped me escape my initial depression and I was fine for about three years. My chemical factory wasn't broke, but it was handicapped leaving me little to no reserve.

Therapy Through Medication

Should you go to a doctor or a psychiatrist for this therapy? Family physicians are a great place to start and they can prescribe some of the medications, but they are limited in what they can do. If you are prescribed drugs for depression, immediately seek out a psychiatrist. These doctors specialize in drugs that affect the mind. There are many different drugs that will affect the mind in different ways and a family physician is not trained to know all of them. Go to the specialist just as you'd go to an oncologist for cancer, an obstetrician for pregnancy or an orthopedic surgeon for bones and joints. For some reason there is a negative thought that goes with the words *shrink* or *psychiatrist*. You think people will say you're crazy! Well you're not crazy; you're depressed and the specialist who treats that disease is a psychiatrist.

My First Experience with Medication

Eventually recognizing the only chance of making it back was to take my supportive wife's advice and see one of those crazy shrinks. Originally, I had put off her recommendation and extended everyone's pain because I didn't understand depression. I didn't understand the role of the psychiatrist and I didn't know there were drugs that could help. Somewhere way down deep, I wanted to get better, but I really had no way of doing it on my own. That thought was the only thing that got me to a psychiatrist. Hopefully with this information, you or someone you know won't hesitate to ask for the help he/she needs; they won't think going to a psychiatrist is a bad thing.

I was given some pills and then I asked what else I needed to do, because I remembered all of those cognitive therapy exercises. The psychiatrist told me I didn't have to do anything. Just give the chemical some time to work. Within a couple days I could peek under that curtain and see there was a possibility of getting out. Within a couple of weeks I started feeling better. With time I could start to interact with people again and I actually was able to laugh. That laughing had been one of the first things to go.

Important: Within about a month, I started feeling almost normal, and unfortunately, I quit taking the medicine because I thought it cured me just as aspirin would cure a headache. This was a bad decision. What happened next was I fell into a depression that was deeper than the one before taking the medication.

When and if you start taking an anti-depressant, do not stop taking it without your doctor's approval. Know what will happen when you quit the drug and know what to look for in your behavior. Have someone else close to you watch your behavior at this time. I personally believe that a lot of suicides in young people come from kids starting on medicine because they were close to or are suicidal and then stopping their medication because they thought they were better. When they stopped, and if they were close to suicide before, taking away the medication could put them over the point of no return. So, if starting medication, don't stop unless your doctor and family know and you should expect to come off of it slowly.

Knowing the Right Drug for You

Prescribing drugs is not an exact science yet and this is another reason to seek the help of a psychiatrist. Everyone is different with a different chemical makeup. I learned at the hospital that one drug might work for you but it might not work for me. Or one drug may work on both of us, but on me it creates a negative side effect. It takes a psychiatrist and patient working together to achieve the best results. My first psychiatrist prescribed one drug and it worked well but I would still periodically fall back into my depression. I then actively went looking for a doctor who would work aggressively with me and tune my medication to find the right drug or drug combination to bring me back to myself. I now use a combination of three drugs to control my depression.

My Stages of Depression

When I was having my medication adjusted, it would take about two weeks to clear one drug from my system and then about another two weeks to feel the effect of the new drug. During this time I went in and out of depression multiple times. Depression seemed to grow worse with each stage. I noticed a pattern of 17 steps in my behavior that occurred with its onset:

1) **Lack of eye contact**: I would not meet someone else's eyes with mine while in a conversation with them. Frequently I'd be looking down. This is the beginning of retreating from a social world. I usually don't recognize it in myself unless I'm looking for it. It's one of my first indicators that things aren't right.
2) **Failure to engage in conversation**: I would never start a conversation and when someone talked to me I would answer quickly and never encourage the conversation to continue.
3) **Anxiety**: A fight or flight feeling. It feels like all the hairs on my body are standing on end or two muscles were pushing against each other. I would feel like my nerves were working against themselves; my mind would want my arm to go up and down at the same time. There would be no motion but my whole body felt like it was fighting itself. It was an exhausting experience.

4) **Solitude**: I would start to seek quiet. It could be my bedroom, a favorite spot in nature, a place where I might go if I just wanted to think. Turning off any music around me was a strong indicator of being in this stage.
5) **Fatigue**: I was beginning to feel tired all of the time. There didn't seem to be any energy to do anything.
6) **Irritability**: I would have a quick temper. Things that I normally did weren't turning out right. I would snap at people without a good reason.
7) **Frustration**: I wasn't happy with anything around me. I couldn't understand where my attitude was coming from and I couldn't seem to change it. A familiar thought was, "Why does this always happen to me?"
8) **Lack of Patience**: The lack of patience would start to build anger. At this point I couldn't understand where the anger was coming from. My lack of patience would be seen when I couldn't tolerate mistakes from people and I would be quick to jump on them with an angry voice.
9) **Anger**: I held onto anger even though there was no reason to be angry. I couldn't seem to shake it. I was angry at everything and everybody and didn't know where the anger was coming from. At this point I could recognize that I was a different person.
10) **Self-Feeding Anger**: Now the anger turned internal. I forgot about where the anger came from and the anger I had would feed upon itself. I was not myself and I became angry that I couldn't be

myself, which built even more rage. At this point, the depression would feed on itself and it would now take outside help to keep from going deeper into this depression.

11) **Despair (Sadness)**: Nothing would make me happy. Music, laughter, hobbies, anything I liked or made me happy just made me sad. I couldn't laugh, it was hard to smile and it was difficult to make conversation. Basically, people could talk at me but I couldn't communicate or explain my sadness. I would quit doing the things that gave me enjoyment and I lost interest in everything.
12) **Awareness**: I noticed that I was affecting the people around me. I would bring them down when they were around me. I recognized the affect I was having on people and it was not the effect I wanted to have. I didn't know how to fix what was happening. I couldn't fix it.
13) **Avoidance**: At this point I recognized I wasn't who I wanted to be and I would avoid people because I thought I was a freak and I didn't want anyone to see me that way. That led to jealousy and envy. When I was around people, I watched them interacting, laughing and having a good time. It hurt to laugh. There was no way to get to the emotion happiness. I literally hated people and so I started to avoid everyone. Whatever came into the mind was skewed. Everything became negative and there was no positive in anything. Like an open sore that is sensitive to touch, emotions are over-

sensitive. I no longer had control over my feelings and little problems became huge.

14) **The Curtain**: This is where my mind just wouldn't function right. I moved into a different place. At this point I saw no way out and the world around me became darker and darker. Everything made me feel sad and I truly felt the emotional pain in trying to deal with this. Many people who have been depressed have described this phase as a big black curtain coming down and it separates you from the world. That's how I felt and I could look out but I couldn't interact. Everything outside of the curtain was untouchable. What comes through is skewed. I couldn't communicate with anyone. I was in a world by myself and I became really alone. In my mind, no one outside of that curtain could understand me. Of course, that wasn't true. I just saw it that way. This world that engulfed me showed no way out and the more I struggled, the deeper it seemed I got.
15) **Isolationism**: I recognized how I affected people and I knew my mind wasn't right. I didn't want to be seen this way (sick) and I didn't want others to be affected by my presence. The only answer was to hide. I wouldn't answer the phone and I wouldn't go out. I only wanted to be some place where I could be left alone. When I slept, there was no pain and no one would bother me, so that seemed to be the answer. I'd go to my bedroom, close the door and sleep and sleep and sleep and

sleep coming out only to eat or go to the bathroom.

16) **Comfort**: There was a point where I became comfortable with myself. I realized and accepted what I was. My world became fine and peaceful as long as everyone left me alone. However, total isolation from people is impossible and so I had to seek another answer.
17) **Suicidal**: Thoughts of suicide would creep into my head. When alone in the quiet, I would think. I'd think about everything. I thought about how unhappy I was with myself. I thought about how unhappy I was making the people around me. So I would think that because I made everybody, including myself, unhappy, why exist? Remember this is a skewed mind trying to rationalize things. At this point I started planning my death.

Suicide is something that is usually thought about for quite some time. During this planning, someone this far into depression may even casually mention that they were thinking of suicide. THIS IS A CALL FOR HELP! They recognize that they can't come out of this by themselves. Without help, or encouragement to seek help, there is only one alternative. Casually mentioning suicide is the *only* tool left to communicate with the outside, saying to them, "I really don't want to die but I have no other choice. Please help me." That call for help is the only thing that can get through that big black curtain.

How Depression Affects People Around You

While in that suicidal state, my wife would come home from work not knowing what to expect. She would become discouraged and angry that I wouldn't help myself by seeing a doctor. There was concern, worry and fear every day. I had no idea how much stress it was putting on her. This was a dark period of my life and it affected the entire family. My kids didn't understand what was going on. Depression wasn't talked about or understood back then.

They would tip-toe around and be very careful not to do anything that would upset me. I had a hair-trigger anger that I tried to keep in check by staying away. So now thoughts of abandonment became a concern for the kids. They couldn't laugh too loud or be rowdy. It just seemed like anything they did upset me. They don't remember seeing me happy at all and I really didn't say much to them. They couldn't bring friends over and because of me they basically couldn't be the kids they should have been.

Depression can hurt strangers as well. There are different ways of ending your own life such as being killed by police for a crime or car accidents. We don't know how many fatal car accidents were really suicide. These examples may get the job done but innocent bystanders may be hurt or killed by being in the wrong place at the wrong time. Someone trying to end it all may have wanted to die but those innocent people caught up in the event surely didn't want to.

I should note here that in the stages of depression come jealousy and anger. And it's an explosive anger. It's bothersome knowing that people can do what you can't. There would be an internal burning rage and you'd know about it but have trouble controlling it. If other people were the initial cause of someone's depression, I can see how that anger could lead to hurting the people who are being blamed for your getting to that state. Remember it is a skewed mind with skewed reasoning and a person in that state can be totally unpredictable. There is no right or wrong in that mind, only pain and anger. My guess would be that this could be the cause of some of these murder suicides such as Columbine.

Recognize Depression in Yourself

If you feel any of the following, you may have depression. If you:

- feel sad all the time or cry for no reason.
- experience emotional pain about the smallest things.
- become angry with yourself, or everyone and everything around you. Your temper is on a hair trigger.
- develop a need to be alone, avoid eye contact, need quiet (no music and sleeping a lot), create strategies to avoid people including lying
- are unable to laugh at anything and happy people have become irritating. You are jealous because you can't enjoy life like everyone else.
- think there is no one you can talk to and no one you can trust. You have thoughts of unfairness and self pity

- realize your emotions are out of control,
- feel isolated like being in a dark hole where you are separated from the human race
- feel your mind and body are trapped in goop with no escape.
- hate what you've changed into
- feel you're a heavy weight on the people around you.
- feel you no longer want to live.

Recognize Depression in Someone Else

It's hardly mentioned but those who have depression can also hide it. They know they aren't behaving right and they don't want anyone to know they are depressed. That person can fake normalcy but can't sustain it. When in the early stages of depression, they would want to isolate themselves. However, there are times that they won't be able to get away from being with people. For me, I could reach down and find enough of something to fake that I was all right. I could muster up what little chemical there was to act normal, at least for a short time.

The down side of this was that it took so much energy to push myself into that normal condition that it cost me dearly and I would isolate myself even more and for a greater length of time. I'm telling you this because when someone is depressed, it isn't always recognizable. A depressed person knows what normal is; it's just that they can't get there and stay there. But they can pull it together it for short periods of time. However, the payback is requiring a longer period of being alone. So if you see someone become isolated after a social event, be suspicious. If the isolation grows longer and longer after they have interacted with people, be concerned. Visual signs of depression could be:

- unusually long periods of isolation - then coming out for short periods of time and acting normal
- periods of isolation becoming longer and longer.
- not wanting to engage in social settings; not wanting to leave the house
- lack of eye contact
- lack of concentration; It seems like they're off in a different world.
- a downward change of personal hygiene
- avoiding music
- an explosive temper
- excessive sleeping
- not laughing
- overeating or under-eating

If you see these behaviors in someone, it may be just a passing depression. However, if you notice that the person can't seem to shake this personality change, help him understand that there can be help if he wants it. Then help guide him to it.

What You Can Do for Someone Who Is Depressed

- *Understand that this is a sickness.*

People do not bring depression upon themselves. This is a disease and it takes lives just like cancer. It just seems that suicide is preventable. If left untreated, *it is not.* There is a downward spiral that leaves no out. The mind skews so many things and personal pain becomes unbearable. I've often said that during depression your emotions become exposed similar to an open cut. Every thing is amplified way out of proportion. When depressed, I knew I was not right but I couldn't fix it. I knew it was affecting the people around me, the people I loved. I didn't want them to suffer any more or tolerate my strange behaviors. When I was suicidal, I ran multiple scenarios through my head thinking that suicide would be the answer for removing pain and stress for a lot of people. I wasn't thinking of the pain, stress and guilt that would occur after my death. This disease robs you of your personality and mind, much like Alzheimer's, however, this one also robs you of your will to live.

- *Learn about depression.*

Try to understand what a depressed person is experiencing. Know that they can't help themselves. My father didn't understand my depression. He didn't think it was a sickness. He would say, "Pick yourself up, get busy and do something, find a job." I knew he didn't understand and so what did I do? I stayed away from him. My wife gathered some educational information and mailed it to him. It made a big difference as to how he viewed me. His perception changed from disgust that I couldn't handle my own problems to love and concern. It brought us a lot closer.

- *<u>Don't pretend to know how that person is feeling.</u>*

"I know what you're going through." A depressed person will take offense to that phrase and resent or hate you for pretending to understand. In a depressed mind, no one can know what he or she is going through. They feel alone in a dark world. How can anyone know what that's like? Another person who is or has been depressed may be able to reach through a little hole in that curtain. Let the depressed person know about some sources of hope and where to find them. My wife would leave the phone number of a psychiatrist around so that when I was ready and strong enough to make the call, it was there. It saved my life.

- *<u>Understand that small could be seen as impossible.</u>*

A small pebble becomes a huge mountain to a depressed person. Just getting out of bed or getting dressed can take monumental effort. So if asked to do something and they don't do it, for the most part it's because they can't. Remember they are not in control of their mind and it's a skewed mind that controls the body. You might not know how much that person is trying to process the request and make the body do as asked. Keep in mind that in this state, there is no right and wrong and there are no consequences worse then what they are experiencing at that time. There is nothing more they can lose by doing nothing.

Be concerned and be watchful.

You can only watch from the sidelines and send in an occasional nudge. If the person doesn't know what clinical depression is, leave a flyer out so that he can learn and understand what he is going through. The depressed person needs to know that it's not his fault. That is the first step to becoming better. Make the path to receiving help easy. Don't push. If it's too hard he won't seek help. It will be done on his time when he is ready and that may only be a small crack in time. That's why the link to help has to be readily available.

- *Take it serious if someone says they want to "end it all".*

Terms like *end it all, want to die, no sense in living,* or *nothing left to live for,* are all catch phrases. If you hear anyone use such a phrase, take it seriously. It is not a call for attention like many people believe it is. A healthy mind would never consider self-destruction. He is in the last stages of depression and is reaching out. Watch him closely and seek help. You may compassionately ask, "If you did kill yourself, how would you do it?" If he returns with a quick answer, that means he's thought of it or even planned it. Acting it out is the next step. So that question might help determine the stage of depression.

If You Know of a Suicide:

The following is a letter I wrote to help a friend through an emotional time because they blamed themselves for allowing someone very close to commit suicide. The death occurred the night after he had asked for his gun back from my friend, who was holding it for him:

He was ready. If not his gun, he would have found another way. Trust me. When I was suicidal I ran multiple scenarios through my head. This is a disease and it takes lives just like cancer. It just seems that suicide is preventable. It is not. There is a downward spiral that leaves no out. The mind skews so many things and personal pain becomes unbearable. I've often said that during depression your emotions become exposed similar to an open cut. Everything is amplified way out of proportion.

This may also help. When depressed, I knew I was not right but I couldn't fix it. I knew it was affecting the people around me, the people I loved. I didn't want them to suffer any more or have them put up with my strange behaviors. When suicidal, I was thinking that I was removing problems for a lot of people. I wasn't even thinking of the problems my death would create.

This disease robs you of your personality and mind, much like Alzheimer's, however this one also robs you of your will to live. The inner man loved you very much or he wouldn't have left a message. I can't tell you the amount of energy it took to reach through this entire muddle of the mind to find his inner self so he could communicate. You lose who you are and you know that. Believe it or not, in his mind, he did this out of love for you, not because of you.

Believe me, this was going to happen no matter what you did or didn't do. Please understand that in his mind, it was an act of love that caused his actions. Also remember how physically sick that mind is. The intensions are right, the actions are wrong.

Try to understand that in a depressed mind, it is usually an act of love that caused the action. The reason I say that is that someone depressed knows how they're affecting the people they love. They think they are the cause of all the pain around them. You could say they love these people so much that they want to remove the pain they are causing them. In truth, to them, it's the ultimate sacrifice. But remember how physically sick that mind is. For a healthy brain, what do you think it would take for someone to want to self-destruct? There is no logic in it. So for the disease called depression, there has to be a chemical short circuit destroying the thought process in that brain.

By Choosing Life, I've Experienced:

- enjoying 16+ yrs of continuing love, compassion, fun and companionship with my incredible wife, my soul mate. There have been trips to Aruba and Hawaii, a cruise ship vacation, and multiple summer trips to a special family cabin on a lake in northern Minnesota.

- becoming a grandfather and watching those beautiful grandchildren grow. Seeing how my life is being carried on from one generation to another is truly amazing. For me to be a part of their lives is something so special, it transcends depression.

- building Wind and Water, which was my windsurfing and kite store for three years. I was able to hire and be responsible for employees. I had articles published in a professional retail magazine. The windsurfing school I started was rated as one of the top in the country. I was on television multiple times. A full-page newspaper article was printed that featured my store. Radio and television personalities became my friends. With the help of a radio station, we sponsored an annual Kite Fest in Des Moines, Iowa. There are a number of people flying kites and sailing windsurfers today who never would have without me.

- making friends with the owners of a company that is the east coast distributor of racing tires. They also maintain and restore vintage racecars. I was asked to develop a computer application to track all the tires, with their various sizes and compounds, sold during the Rolex Daytona 24 hour race. I actually ran the application for them right in the pit area next to the teams and engineers who came from all over the world. Working with all of the exotic, multimillion-dollar cars and teams, was a thrill that can't be put into words.

- driving a NASCAR racecar at 147 mph at Lowe's Motor Speedway.

- finding and buying a beautiful piece of property on a lake in North Carolina. On that property I built our dream retirement home. In doing so I became proficient in framing, shingling, plumbing, electrical, tiling and cabinetry. It is a home built out of love and passion and extreme attention to detail. Many have admired my work and it will become part of my legacy.

- designing an electro-mechanical computerized switch. I now have a patent for that switch. Going through that whole process was quite an education.

- kite boarding and because I'm an old athlete, I learned that I have to be in some kind of condition for this extreme sport. I'm working at getting back into shape so I can control the kite instead of the kite controlling me.

- helping people understand depression so they can live a normal life again. I don't want anyone to learn the lessons as I did--the hard way. Even though I'm still living with depression, my circle of friends has grown to a point I never could have imagined.

- writing this book and educating people about depression. Taking my story to print will be another legacy of mine.

So, has living made a difference? If I had taken my life, all of my experiences past that time would never have happened. All of the people with whom I have interacted would have never met me. I will now leave legacies behind, including the impact that my living has on my grandchildren.

Remember, the future is unknown. If you're depressed, know that there are so many good things out there that *you will* experience. ***The good in the future will far outweigh anything that is happening now***. You can't think straight when you're depressed. First you have to get that depression down to a controllable level. Seeing a professional will help to do that. If you are not depressed, please help those who are. You'll need love, patience and an understanding of this disease called depression to do that.

As a final note, I want to add one more story. One Sunday during the middle of my dark time, my wife took me to church at Boys Town in Omaha, Nebraska. As part of the service we stood and I had to, with great fear, face a stranger. He shook my hand and said to me, "Peace be with you." He didn't know I had depression, but when he said those words, I experienced the feeling that my dark demons were being pulled from me. I gained that little piece of hope that there was a way out. I hope this book will give comfort, understanding and hope to those who need it.

If you are reading this book and have depression, fight your way out. With whatever you have left inside, find that crack in the curtain and fight your way through it. You can't see it now but looking back, you will be so glad you did.

Peace be with you.

Don Legun

I am not a doctor or psychologist and the information I've provided is my insight based upon my experiences. It has not been approved or supported by any medical or psychological organization.

To Our Service Men and Women

I want to honor those men and women who have come back from war and are carrying the burden of clinical depression. All military personnel need to know that depression is not a disease of choice. When fighting a war, duty and honor may come in direct conflict with one's conscience and morals. This kind of conflict usually is the beginning of clinical depression. This disease is real, physical, and caused by a chemical deficiency inside the brain. Sustained, it will leave a person as crippled as an amputee. Prosthetics and therapy help an amputee to live a normal life. For depression, the prosthetic is the chemicals that the brain no longer has. It takes therapy and time to fit the chemicals to individual minds. A prosthetic (material or chemical) is what helps the wounded soldier be productive again.

The military trains the body to be strong. Yet there is no basic training that makes the mind strong to absorb the horrors of war. When clinical depression happens, no matter how much any superior wants it, it cannot be willed away. Yelling and discipline can make a situation worse. We are taught how to put pressure on an open wound to stop bleeding. We are not taught how to handle the wound of depression. Mistreatment of either situation can result in death.

For anyone coming home not feeling mentally right, understand that this is a physical problem not an emotional one. It isn't a case of not being able to handle your own problems. Time alone will not heal clinical depression. Without balancing the chemicals of the mind, an altered personality can become unrecognizable--resulting in loss of family, friends or life. Like diabetes, a depressed body needs chemical therapy. Since the chemicals for depression are in the brain, go to the doctor that specializes in those chemicals, a psychiatrist. **Don't let anybody tell you seeing a psychiatrist is a sign of weakness.** It is your source of healing.

My message to senior military personnel is to recognize and treat clinical depression as a physical wound. It is not a wound of choice; like shrapnel or a bullet, it is inflicted upon an individual. The entire military needs education to recognize depression and know what to do when around it. The person with it does not want it. Without proper education, clinical depression can be mishandled and the results may end up as suicide, murder or both. Lastly, don't shame or belittle these wounded troops as was done with me. Respect them and their injury. **Fitness Reports and Evaluations should not reflect depression as a weakness but instead as an injury**. These brave troops are going through torture unbeknown to those who have never experienced it. Although controllable, this injury is lasting. If brought about by military events, this chemical injury to the brain should be worthy of a Purple Heart.

I hope all military personnel read this book because you can't fight the enemy until you understand it. Like cancer, clinical depression takes lives. Like Alzheimer's, clinical depression is a chemical problem of the brain. Depression needs to be recognized for the disease it is. Educate yourself and know that improper interaction can create escalation. Finally, whether it is you or someone you know, ensure that help is found.

Sources for Help

Immediate Help

Covenant House Nineline
800 999-9999 www.nineline.org
Great Support, Immediate Help-24 hr

Boys Town National Hotline
800 448-3000 www.boystown.org
Immediate Help-24 hr, Good Parental Support

National Suicide Prevention_Talkline
800 273-8255
Immediate Help-24 hr

Yellow Ribbon
www.yellowribbon.org
Can locate local chapters, Good source for person to person help

For Frequently Asked Questions

www.mentalhealthamerica.net/go/information/faqs:
Good source of info if you know someone in trouble, go here

For Teens To Learn More

www.mpoweryouth.org
Designed for Teens, Musicians and Bands that recognize youth problems and want to help

www.mpoweryouth.org/411HelpWhere.htm
A section designed for someone to get help & provides answers to FAQs

www.mpoweryouth.org/411ReadStory.htm
Actual stories that you might relate to

www.mentalhealthamerica.net/reallives
Actual stories that you might relate to

Other Sources of Information

Families for Depression Awareness
www.familyaware.org
Great source of depression information, it's well laid out and expert advice sections, for teens, parents or care givers

Suicide Prevention Resource Center
www.sprc.org
Good information for care givers be it teens, teachers, parents or others

UCLA Clearinghouse
http://smhp.psych.ucla.edu/qf/depression.htm
Source of books on child and adolescent depression

Columbia University
www.teenscreen.org
Screening of teens with mental health issues

Depression & Bipolar Support Alliance
www.dbsalliance.org
Good source of info for Bipolar, Deals with suicide and provides good links

Righter Publishing Company

Fresh, delightful stories for the modern reader.

Local histories, family histories, thrillers, detective stories, short story collections, children's books, inspirational books, poetry collections, science fiction, romance and personal memoirs

Go to www.righterbooks.com

Made in the USA
Monee, IL
04 November 2026

67383425R00036